Encounters with Rabbits

OR

Critters, a Cross, and a Cemetery

by

Niki Thornock

ISBN: 978-1-7365272-0-7

Layout design by Niki Thornock

Cover design and main cover photos by Sky Evans

1949 Easter Cross photo used by permission

Other photos taken by Niki Thornock

Cover font set in Chaparral Pro; text font set in 11 pt Georgia

Every city has a cemetery. Death is a part of life and people need a place to go when they die. I knew that Provo, Utah had a public cemetery, but I didn't know it had a private cemetery until I went actively looking for one.

Established in 1954, the EastLawn Memorial Hills Cemetery is not one you would stumble across while driving around the city. It's tucked away in the foothills, partway up Cascade Mountain, with a beautiful view of the valley. After winding your way up the quarter-mile driveway, it's kind of a surprise to come around the corner and see all of that land spread out before you.

The cemetery is 25 acres in size and most of it is lawn. All of the headstones are flush with the ground so the lawn mower can go right over the top of them. Trees and stone benches line the perimeters of the various areas. Small flowerbeds abound.

Separation of church and state prohibits religious symbols in a public cemetery, but that doesn't apply here. There's a statue of Jesus, a mural of the Last Supper, a giant stone rendering of the Lord's Prayer, and a ten-foot masonry cross called the Easter Cross (my contribution, and why I was looking for a private cemetery).

Then, there are the rabbits. Everyone who visits the cemetery notices the semi-tame rabbits hopping around the various areas. If you mention EastLawn Cemetery, people will either say, "Where is that?" or "The one with all the rabbits?" The rabbits each have their own places where they like to gather.

A couple of them hang out under the trees by the road on the east side of the cemetery. Another one likes the bushes at the north end of the cemetery. There's usually at least one that likes to hang around the office building, which is in the middle of the cemetery.

The south half of the office building looks like an office, with a computer desk and chairs, and couches for people to sit on when they come to buy a burial plot from the cemetery. A binder is kept on the desk with the names of the people who are buried here, and where their graves are located. The door between the south half and the north half of the office is kept closed when people are visiting.

The north half of the building looks like a work room, which it is. It has a break room for the employees, supplies, file cabinets full of old records, and all sorts of equipment: Lawn-care equipment, watering cans, lots of sprinkler heads and parts and paraphernalia, tools for repairing the lawn mowers, gas cans, hoses, and more. It also has measuring equipment, so that when the full-time employees dig a grave with the backhoe, they can be sure to dig in the right place.

A few bronze headstones are kept under the workbench. They have individual letters, so the cemetery can provide a temporary headstone for each funeral service, complete with the name of the person being buried. These headstones are different for men, women, and children.

The land to the north and east (and part of the west) of the cemetery is untamed mountain, so you can often see wild animals in the cemetery. Squirrels and lizards scamper around. Magpies and gray jays flutter around the trees and bushes. Hawks soar overhead. Deer graze around the perimeter and sometimes into the cemetery.

Some years, a flock of wild turkeys wanders around. One year, three owls (two parents and a chick) built a nest high in a tree at the south side of the cemetery. The supervisor told me about staying after dark and seeing a bobcat in the middle of the road. Another time, he ran into a rattlesnake.

There's a peace about the cemetery. It's far above the city, so most of the sounds are natural. It's big enough that you can almost always find a quiet place, and there are lots of benches and grass to sit on. The employees work hard to keep the grass green (something of a challenge in this climate) and mowed, and the flower beds clean and weeded. It's a good place to rest and relax in peace.

Encounters with Rabbits

Although every city has a cemetery, people pay very little attention to them unless it's Memorial Day or a loved one has passed on. Most people are unaware of the small industry that goes into action when somebody passes away. I was equally unaware until I started working at a cemetery.

I did not set out to find work at EastLawn Cemetery. I set out to find a home for a ruined religious monument that had been forgotten for 40 years. I was offered a job because I was there when they needed a hand.

In the following pages, I weave together stories about how a cemetery works, the big stone cross that sent me looking for a private cemetery, and my encounters with rabbits and other critters.

* * * * *

There is almost always at least one rabbit hanging around the office.

One day, I went into the office and found a big bunch of balloons. Rather unusual for a cemetery.

"Somebody's birthday?" I asked.

"It's the rabbit's birthday," the supervisor said with a twinkle. "We're giving them to him."

We finished the conversation and I opened the back door to find the rabbit sitting on the doormat, looking at me. I stared at it for a minute.

"The rabbit is here for his balloons," I called back into the office[1].

The supervisor started to laugh. "Send him in!"

[1] Someone had brought the balloons for the sexton (or manager).

* * * * *

I originally went looking for a private cemetery because I was trying to find a place to rebuild an old religious monument called the Easter Cross. It was a ten-foot masonry cross that had been built in the foothills of Y Mountain in 1939 for a yearly interdenominational Easter sunrise service[1].

The cross was built by stonemason Nathan Dixie Hiatt[2]. The services were started by the Provo Community Congregational Church, as it was known at that time. The sunrise services ended in 1951 because of the unpredictable spring weather conditions. The cross stood for a couple of decades before vandals tore it down

in the 1970s. It lay forgotten on Y Mountain for the next 40 years.

Around 2014, my neighbor showed me a picture of herself sitting on the cross in 1949. Then she showed me the remains on Y Mountain. It felt so wrong to have something that important to so many people lying forgotten in ruins that I decided to get it rebuilt. But that was a lot easier said than done, and people had been saying it for at least 10 years[3].

I didn't really know how to start. I decided that whatever I did should be legal, so I needed to talk to the property owner. How does one track down the owner of a brush-and-rock-covered piece of mountainside?

I had an advantage in this case because about ten years ago, I had worked as a secretary to an appraiser and had learned how to use the online county land records and parcel map. I went up to the cross and looked around enough to identify where it was. Then I found it using the satellite images on the parcel map. The parcel map gave me the parcel number and the land records gave me the owner's name and contact info. I called and asked him about rebuilding the cross. He said he was busy right then, but I should call him back in a month, with a plan, and he would see what he could do.

Over the course of the next month, I got bids on reconstructing the cross from a couple of stonemasons and found a structural engineer to design a base for it. I planned to use crowdfunding to raise the money for the stonemason because I couldn't afford it on my own. I wanted the donations to be tax deductible so I asked an interdenominational group if I

could collect donations through them. They agreed. Things were lining up nicely.

When the month was over, I called the property owner again. He was fine with the plan. He said I could have the cross, but I couldn't rebuild it where it was. He planned to develop the property and didn't want to have to work around the cross. So I needed to find another place to put it. When I asked the interdenominational group for their tax ID, which was required by the crowdfunding website, they said they couldn't share it with anyone outside of their organization. They would not be able to help me.

Back to square one.

[1] Carter, D. Robert, "Worshipping at the Easter Cross," Provo Daily Herald, 27 March 2005.

[2] Evidence of this was given to the author by his grandchildren.

[3] Opinion, "Restore the Easter Cross," Provo Daily Herald, 15 April 2004, p. A6.

* * * * *

The cemetery hosts a number of funeral services each week. The service procedure generally starts with a call from the mortuary. They tell us who died, whom to contact, the date and time of the service, and the location of the burial plot, if there is one. If not, the family needs to come up and pick one out. This (and other) information is typed up and put on a clipboard on the wall. The wall has a column for every day of the week, except Sunday, when we're closed.

A day or two before the service, a couple of full-timers take the measuring tape and the backhoe out to the plot listed on the clipboard. The cemetery is divided into hundreds of sections, and each section holds 32 plots. They check and measure to make sure that they are in the correct spot. (This also means that they're less likely to hit a sprinkler pipe while digging.)

They use shovels to cut the sod that covers the spot and move it to the side. Then the supervisor uses the backhoe to dig a hole for the grave and puts the dirt into a dump truck. The hole is three-and-a-half feet wide by eight-and-a-half feet long and five-and-a-half feet deep. (Double deep is nine feet.) Depending on the size of the hole, they might need to empty the dump truck over by the compost yard.

Some of the vehicles, like the battery-powered cart and the pickup truck, are light enough that they won't damage the headstones, if they drive over them. The dump truck, the backhoe, and the funeral-setup truck are all big enough that they could crack a headstone, if we're not careful. So we're careful.

Any time we're preparing for a service, the full-timers load a dozen or so 4×8-foot sheets of plywood onto the back of the pickup. They try to pick a path to the grave site that passes over the fewest headstones. Then they place a sheet of plywood over each headstone in the path. The plywood distributes the weight of the truck so it's less likely to damage the headstone.

Once the hole is finished, they put a two-by-four plank over the hole and cover it with a couple more pieces of plywood. (The two-by-four keeps the plywood from falling into the hole.) They put a bright yellow cone on top of the plywood and a couple more cones by the

road close to the site to reserve a parking space for the hearse. They gather up the plywood that covered the headstones. Then, that job is done, until the funeral service is over and the casket and vault are in the hole.

At that point, they bring over a dump truck full of dirt and refill the hole (after laying down the plywood again). They usually dump the right amount, but sometimes they end up shoveling dirt into or out of the hole. They add water and pack the dirt down as much as they can to reduce the amount of settling. They put the sod back over the hole and soak it thoroughly. They put a temporary bronze headstone on the sod, along with a small metal-and-plastic marker with the person's name, and arrange all of the funeral flowers around the headstone.

The headstone might stay there for a day or so, depending on the number of services and how soon it's needed again. The metal-and-plastic marker stays there until the family buys a headstone. (Sometimes the mortuary provides a nicer marker with a picture.) The family is usually advised to wait about six months to give the dirt time to settle, so the headstone doesn't sink into the ground. However, we have some metal-and-plastic markers that are 10 to 15 years old.

The flowers are cleaned up after about a week, and only the freshly moved sod shows that there was a recent burial.

* * * * *

One day, my son and I were out walking in the cemetery. A large brown hawk swooped overhead with a loud "KEE-yaahhhhh!" My son jumped. "Mommy, I want to hear the hawk quack again!" For the next few years, our running joke was that hawks quacked.

A couple of years later, I was busy weeding when I realized that a hawk had been screaming at regular intervals for the last several minutes. I got out my phone and recorded a few minutes of hawk calls. My son was thrilled.

* * * * *

I spent the next several months trying to find another place to put the Easter Cross. I wanted to keep it close to the original location, or at least on the same mountain. Most of the mountain was either residential or undeveloped.

Also, there was a locked gate at the foot of the road that led to the cross. Bikes and pedestrians could pass, but cars could not. There weren't many good places near the road where I could build the cross, and farther away was harder to get to.

I found one possible location on a part of the mountain that was owned by the local university. I explained the history and asked for permission to rebuild the cross there. After "careful deliberation," they said no. I eventually concluded that the people who were most likely to remember the cross and want to visit it were less likely to be able to climb a mountain to get there. I needed to find a more accessible location.

Whenever I mentioned that I was looking for a place to put the cross, someone would suggest a city park. Unfortunately, the current interpretation of separation of church and state means no religious symbols on public property. A cross is unquestionably a religious symbol. So I started looking at religious properties. I got a list of all of the religious organizations in the area from the interdenominational group and started working my way through it.

First, I ruled out the religions that did not use the cross as part of their worship. Then I looked at the addresses on an online map, and ruled out the ones that were meeting in rented buildings. Then I started contacting people.

One particularly promising church, which a friend attended, had a large property; but I couldn't seem to get anywhere with them. The friend regularly forgot to ask, then the pastor was extremely busy, then the church committee was unavailable, and then they got a new pastor. I gave up after a few months and continued down the list.

My usual tactic was to check the church's website for Bible study times or office hours. Then I paid them a visit to ask if they had room for a cross. The preacher/priest/official was invariably polite and kind and friendly, and said they would need to talk to their committee and get back to me. How soon depended on when the committee was meeting next. Then they would call or email me a week or three later and say that the answer was no.

After about nine months, I had worked my way through the entire list, without success. I was running out of ideas. The only property I owned was where my house was. If I rebuilt the cross there, the next owner would almost certainly tear it down.

Encounters with Rabbits

I was getting pretty discouraged. I talked to my mom about the problem, and she asked why I was doing this. I told her that I just wanted the cross to have a place to rest in peace. She suggested a cemetery. The public cemetery was obviously out. That's when I discovered that Provo had a private cemetery.

I called the owner of EastLawn Cemetery and asked about the cross. He remembered the Easter Cross from before it was ruined and agreed to give me space for it. I was immensely relieved and overjoyed. Then there was the question of exactly where to put it. We spent an hour wandering all over the cemetery.

As we walked along a terrace on the west side of the cemetery, we found two large rabbits having a face-off. They stared at each other from about six feet apart and were sort of shuffling their feet. Then they both leaped four feet in the air

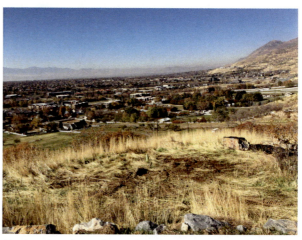

(ka-pwing!) and traded places. The cemetery owner jumped too, but not so high. They shuffled a bit more and leaped again. They were still shuffling and leaping when we continued on our way.

We finally settled on a small piece of un-developed land, just past the retaining wall at

14

the north edge of the cemetery. It had a few scrub oak trees and a lot of dead grass, thistles, rocks, and bushes. I was one step closer to done.

* * * * *

Memorial Day weekend is the biggest event of the year for the cemetery. All of the employees work hard to make sure that the cemetery is as nice as possible because thousands of people will be coming. The lawn is mowed, the headstones are edged, and lots of weeds are pulled.

The cemetery provides hundreds of white wooden crosses on metal stakes with an American flag on top of them. People can take them and put them wherever they want in the cemetery.

We put No Parking signs on one side of the road so people will park on the other and cars can still get past. We set up water taps all over the cemetery; usually there's just the one by the office. We clean the bird droppings off the statue of Jesus and polish the bronze. Everyone is kind of stressed, especially the supervisor.

The sexton frequently orders a new American flag around then because the old one gets kind of ragged at the edges. The flag hangs right at the west edge of the cemetery, overlooking the valley. You can see the flag from the valley, if you know where to look[1].

A few people come on Wednesday, Thursday, and Friday to avoid the rush on Saturday, Sunday, and Monday. That's when mobs of people come to put flowers (and other things) on the graves. All of the full-timers are there over the weekend. They help people find graves.

Encounters with Rabbits

(They usually start by looking up the name in the directory and marking the location on a map. Sometimes they take the person out to the area.) They stock the white crosses. They direct people to the various water sources.

Everything stays pretty much where it is for the next week. We run some of the sprinklers, but the lawn doesn't get mowed because it's covered by all of the flowers and other things. The Monday after Memorial Day (as clearly posted on several signs) is clean-up day. If anyone wants to keep their decorations, they had better pick them up before Monday. We frequently collect all of the white crosses on Friday or Saturday, so there's less to pick up on Monday.

On Monday morning, the full-timers and I, and anybody else we can arrange to bring, grab a plastic garbage can and work our way from one end of the cemetery to the other. High-quality items, like glass vases, figurines, artificial flowers, pinwheels, stuffed animals, and plastic toys, are set at the edge of the lawn for people to pick up.

Everything else is thrown away; things like dying flowers, pictures, paper items, candy, and soft drinks. They are usually in pretty bad shape after sitting in the sun and the sprinklers for a week. The few potted flowers that are still in good condition are set aside for planting. We fill up the garbage cans and then empty them into a huge high-sided trailer for transport to the dump. This is hot and tiring and usually takes until mid-afternoon.

One clean-up day, I picked up a potted chrysanthemum and found a baby rabbit. It was hiding in the shade of the flower to avoid the sun (which tells you how small the rabbit was). We left the flower there for a while, but it was odd to look across the empty lawn and see one lone flower. I eventually went back, picked up the flower, and encouraged the rabbit to hide in the shade of the big pine tree nearby. It stayed there for most of the day.

[1] Drive east on Orem Center Street. As you're descending toward the Shops at Riverwoods, look up at the mountain. The Easter Cross is to the left of the flag. Late afternoon is the best time to see the Cross.

* * * * *

I spent the next several months trying to raise money to rebuild the cross. I passed out flyers to several hundred people, and asked businesses, philanthropists, historical organizations, churches on the interdenominational list, and anyone else I could think of for help or donations. Almost everyone said no.

One historical organization said that they would be willing to help if I left the cross in its original location. Unfortunately, the new place could not be considered a historic site, so they couldn't help.

One group that was willing to help was the church that started the sunrise services that led to the construction of the Easter Cross: the Provo Community Congregational United Church of Christ. They did not have space to rebuild the cross, but they did allow me to go through them to set up the crowdfunding. It took several emails and a few visits to the meet-and-greet after their Sunday service, but we finally arranged it.

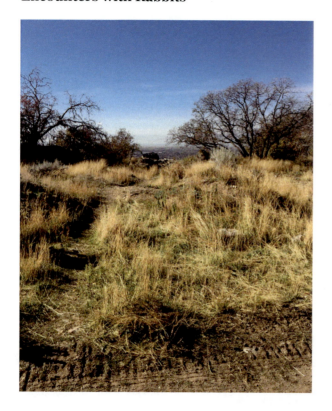

The other project in the works was transporting the cross from the mountain to the cemetery. The cross was about 80 feet from the road, with several erosion barriers that looked like skiing moguls in the way. I contacted a few crane companies to see if they could lift the cross out. Most of them did not have the very large crane needed to reach that far from the road. Also, a crane that size would have a hard time making its way up the winding asphalt and dirt roads to get to the cross location. The crane operators declined.

A friend pointed out that if we could find a large bulldozer to carry the cross, he could use his Bobcat skid-steer to clear the erosion barriers out of the way. Rather surprisingly, I found a bulldozer through the local university. Then we had to make arrangements with the property owner to get a key to the gate at the foot of the hill. We had to sign some paperwork for liability purposes, and we promised to put back the erosion barriers.

A few days before we planned to make the move, I got an email from the property owner. He had been looking over the location with a friend, and the friend pointed out that moving heavy equipment into the mountains in Utah in July was a fire hazard. Sparks and hot machinery had been known to start wildfires. The owner did not want to deal with that and asked us to postpone the move until the fall, when the weather was cooler.

I went back to fundraising.

* * * * *

I was in the southeast corner of the cemetery, watering blue-flowered caryopteris shrubs.

These had been planted recently to replace some small mugo pine trees that the deer had taken a liking to. A wall of pyracantha bushes and pine and willow trees runs for a couple hundred yards along the east side of the cemetery, separating the lawn from the driveway. Three rabbits were browsing on the lawn near the bushes. In a swirl of brown and white feathers, a hawk dove after one of the rabbits. (I had seen its brown-and-white-barred belly and the bottom of its wings.) The rabbit took off running and they both disappeared into the bushes.

I watched for a few seconds, half expecting to see the hawk flap out of the bushes carrying the rabbit. About 15 seconds later, they both burst out of the bushes about 20 feet farther along and went back in again. I could hear the quail pipping nervously. After another 15 or 20 seconds, the hawk swirled out and went back

in again. It eventually came out again, empty clawed, and flew up to land in a tree. No dinner this time.

* * * * *

I had wondered for a while what happened after the full-timers dug a hole for a service. One day, I got a chance to find out. A funeral-setup truck arrived about the time I finished watering, so I decided to go see what was going on. (I did not count my watching time as working time.)

When I arrived at the grave site, the full-timers had hauled off the plywood they used to cover the hole and the setup guy was busily working. He had put one aluminum plank at each end of the hole and two aluminum planks on each side. (The hole is a rectangle.) The planks were about a foot wide and 10 feet long. The side planks were on top of the end planks, making a sort of platform. He used a spirit level to make sure the platform was flat. Then he added a couple of metal supports for the vault.

Most people who have been to a funeral know what a casket is. It's the box that the deceased person lays in; it usually has a hinged lid. A vault is a concrete box that is built to hold a casket; its lid comes completely off. The vault is frequently painted or otherwise finished to look nice. The one I observed was white with gold trim. The vault supports look kind of like bicycle handle bars. The handles are on the platform and the middle drops down about a foot, so the vault is suspended above the hole. (If the vault just looks like concrete, they put it all the way in the hole.)

After the setup guy put in the vault supports, he covered the platform with carpets of

artificial grass (called 'greens'). This is what the pallbearers walk on when they're putting the casket over the hole. Then he set about moving the vault.

A funeral-setup truck is sort of a cross between a flatbed truck and a crane because it needs to both haul and move the vault. The vault is extremely heavy, as might be expected of a concrete box that size. Support wires were wrapped around the vault, so he attached them to the hook at the end of the crane. He had already put down the outriggers, which hold the truck steady.

Then came the tricky part. The hole was directly under a big scrub oak tree, and the setup guy had been given instructions not to break the tree. He had to maneuver the crane beam and vault directly over the hole, while avoiding the various branches.

It took me a while to figure out how he was controlling the crane because all of his attention was on the vault and the tree. He had a remote control in one hand and was using his thumb to control six different up-down switches. He successfully got the vault onto the supports without breaking any branches. He did dislodge a few clumps of leaves and a couple of showers of acorns. (He commented that it felt like a hailstorm. He was standing under the tree so he could see the hole. I was back out of the way.)

After the vault was down, he unhooked the support wires and exchanged the single hook for a quad hook. He placed all four hooks into loops on the lid of the vault. Then he lifted the lid (with the crane, still dodging the tree) and leaned it on a metal sawhorse so it faced where the service would be held. (If the lid looks like concrete, it goes back on the truck.) He swung the crane back to its rest position, lifted the outriggers, and moved the truck away from the hole. (I shoved the lid. It did not budge.) Then he swept the leaves and acorns out of the vault.

At that point, he got what looked like weather-stripping and ran it all the way around the lip of the vault. He would remove the paper lining just before he put the lid on, and it would create an air-tight seal around the vault. He handed me a piece of the sealant. It was kind of like play-dough made of tar.

Then he got out four gadgets whose bottoms fit neatly over the corners of the vault and whose tops looked like dinner plates. He put the casket-lowering device on top of those.

The casket-lowering device (that's its real name) is a rectangle of chrome-plated poles.

Encounters with Rabbits

The corners are shiny round cylinders about six inches tall. It has two green straps that the casket sits on. The setup guy spent a few minutes adjusting the straps so they were rolled neatly, and tightening the poles. Then he put some casket placer roller bars on top of the lowering device. (Yes, I did have to look that up.) These allow the casket to be rolled (rather than lifted) into place.

He put the name plate on the lid (it lists the deceased person's name) and used some sealant to hold it in place. The name plate was about four or five inches high, two feet wide, and half-an-inch thick. It looked like shiny gold and felt like rubber. Then he went off to set up the awning.

* * * * *

The weather had cooled down in October, but it was November before we made arrangements to move the cross. We needed to coordinate with the property owner to get the key to the gate, the bulldozer to move the cross, and my friend to clear the way.

Sometime in October, I went with a stonemason to look at the cross, to get a bid for repairing it. I was shocked to find that the top surface of the cross had been spray-painted completely black. I had cleaned off some random graffiti earlier, but this was something else entirely. Also, it was a further confirmation that the Easter Cross needed to be moved.

One Monday morning, my friend and I went up and he used his skid-steer to clear the erosion barrier so the bulldozer could get through when it came on Tuesday. While we were there, we decided to see if the skid-steer could lift one of the pieces of the cross, although it seemed unlikely. It turned out that it could, so he hauled the piece out by the road. The second piece looked heavier, but the skid-steer managed that too. He also hauled over some bushel baskets of rocks, a.k.a. building material, that I had collected. I didn't know if we would have enough stone for the repair and I didn't think we could get the key to the gate again.

We took a lunch break then, so my friend could go and get his big trailer. We hadn't expected to need one until Tuesday. We loaded everything onto the trailer and strapped it down. I called the bulldozer guy and told him he wouldn't be needed. Then my friend began the tedious process of reconstructing the erosion barrier. He said that he would have made the path a lot narrower if he had known that we wouldn't need the bulldozer.

When he was done, I raked the dirt smooth and scattered a bunch of grass seed. Then we hauled the cross over to the cemetery.

It was getting late, so we left the trailer there overnight. The next morning, we hauled the pieces of the cross to their new home, just off the north end of the cemetery.

* * * * *

I do a lot of weeding. In a place with lots of small gardens, weeds are always growing. So I find an overgrown place and clean it up. A few weeks later, it needs cleaned up again.

My number-one tool for weeding is a long-handled shovel (or spade). I place the shovel next to a weed, then drive the shovel into the ground with my foot. I pull back on the shovel handle, which lifts the dirt, push the shovel handle back to vertical, and remove the shovel. Then I move to the next weed (or the width of the shovel) and repeat the process. I do this in a row for about six feet.

Then I set the shovel down and go back to the beginning of the row. I kneel down on a knee pad (saves my knees and keeps most of the dirt off my pants) and grab the trowel (mini hand-shovel). I drive the trowel into the dirt, push down on the handle, and pick the weeds off the top of the dirt with my other hand. (This doesn't work very well if I haven't already used the big shovel.)

Definition: Weed. A plant that's growing where I don't want it to grow.

I drop the weeds in a bucket that I keep next to me. Once I have pulled up all of the weeds that I can easily reach, I move over a foot or two and pull up the weeds over there. I move the bucket over with me, so it's always within easy reach.

If a weed snaps off or won't come out, I make a note of it and keep on going. When I reach the end of the part that has been dug up, I set down the trowel and pick up the shovel again. I dig deeper near the weeds that wouldn't come up. Then I dig another row. A friend once referred to this process as "scorched-earth weeding."

Once I have finished weeding an area, I rake it smooth. The dirt gets loosened by the shovel, and then packed down by my knees, so it looks pretty lumpy.

The area looks really nice for a week or so, and then the weeds start to crop up again.

* * * * *

Encounters with Rabbits

One year, a large brownish-gray rabbit started hanging around the office. It would curl up in the shade and watch everyone walk around. One day, it dug a hole in the flowerbed next to the front door of the office and made an awful mess of the flowers. We filled in the hole and cleaned up the mess. A day or two later, it dug another hole in the same place and started collecting large mouthfuls of dried grass. Mama Rabbit was making a nest.

We didn't want a nest right where visitors were walking in, so I waited until the rabbit was out of the hole and then collapsed the tunnel, hoping she would switch to Plan B. That might have been a mistake. Plan B was inside the north end of the office. She had picked a spot under a shelf in the storage room. We kept the office doors shut (with her outside) and hoped she would switch to Plan C.

A few days later, I walked into the north end of the office and just about jumped out of my skin. A tiny pink-and-white baby rabbit was crawling blindly around the floor. Its eyes were still shut and its ears were flat back to its head. It was crawling on its elbows and knees, as it were, because its feet weren't active yet.

I stared at it, thinking, "What is this and where did it come from and how did it get here and what am I supposed to do with it?" After a minute, I calmed down enough to realize that Mama Rabbit had stuck with Plan B.

The baby was making fairly good progress, bumping into walls and buckets, but it was traveling away from the nest. I spotted Mama Rabbit outside, so I walked around to her far side, hoping she would go inside, pick up the baby like a mother cat, and take it back to the

nest. She hopped into the office, sniffed the baby a few times, and came back outside again.

I went back in and grabbed a dustpan and the nearest thing handy, which turned out to be a pair of pliers. Then I carefully moved the baby into the dustpan and deposited it back under the shelf.

The babies spent the next couple of weeks in the storage room, getting bigger and furrier. There were nine of them; half a dozen were white and the others were black, brownish-gray, and tan. I lost track of them for a day or so when they moved under the next shelf.

They liked to curl up in a heap in corners, behind the fridge, next to the feed bag, etc. Eventually their interest expanded and they started wandering around the rest of the office.

They scampered away whenever someone approached.

Their next stage was venturing out the back door. One of them hid under the battered old pickup truck parked by the door. I needed to take the pickup, so I stomped my feet to try to scare the rabbit. It didn't move. I started the engine, but it still didn't come out from under the truck. I backed up very, very slowly to give it time to move away from the wheels, if necessary. I was relieved when I got back far enough to see that it was still alive and well.

Three weeks after I found the baby crawling blindly on the floor, I came into the office to find that the babies had left the nest. They were scattered around outside. Somebody had thoroughly cleaned the storage room. After that, we found them hopping in and out of the grass, bushes, flower beds, office, and bathroom, and hiding in random corners and under various vehicles.

* * * * *

Finding a place to put the Easter Cross was not the last step in the process. I still needed to landscape the area, find a stonemason to rebuild the cross, and collect enough money to pay the stonemason.

A Boy Scout in my area was looking for an Eagle project, so he took on the task of putting in sprinklers and laying sod around the cross. We consulted with a landscaper to make the design. A sort of driveway sloped down from the cemetery proper to the cross area. A big clump of scrub oak grew on one side of the slope. The cemetery retaining wall was on the other.

I cleared out the weeds and the brush. We decided to leave most of the scrub oak. The cemetery compost yard was not too far from the cross area, which was just as well, because I had to make a lot of trips.

On the day of the Eagle project, we dug a trench for the sprinkler pipes, installed sprinklers, leveled the ground, and laid sod on the slope and in the cross area. We had a lot of help, but it still took all day. (I was not a cemetery employee at this point.) The landscape design had called for shrubs around the perimeter, but the sod cost so much that we decided not to do them. One clump of trees was perfectly suited to shade a bench, but that was also out of the budget.

Over the next several months, I weeded the area around the sod several times. I eventually laid more sod around the perimeter. I also cleaned the dead wood out of the scrub oak patch. (Scrub oak grows in clumps because the tree roots are interconnected. The roots mostly grow sideways, not down.)

The landscape by the cross area was coming along nicely. However, I still didn't have a stonemason to rebuild the cross; or, more importantly, a way to pay him.

* * * * *

Once the hole and the vault are ready, the funeral-setup guy sets up the awning. The awning is a fifteen-foot-square tent. It keeps the weather off the people attending the service. The frame was made up of four tripods (with three legs) and one with four legs. The legs are about seven-and-a-half feet long. The tripods form the corners of the awning. One leg is on

the ground and the other two are in the air. The tripods form the four corners.

The setup guy lifted up one leg from one tripod and hooked it to a leg from another tripod to make a 15-foot pole that formed one side of the awning. He did this with the other tripods and had a square frame seven feet in the air. He spent some time making sure that the frame was exactly square.

Then he got out a dark-blue canvas cover and spread it out on the ground in the middle of the frame. Each tripod has a four-inch spike at the top of it. Each corner of the cover has a reinforced hole. He put the holes in the canvas over the spikes on the tripods to hold them in place. Once the cover was hooked over the poles, he looped the straps on the inside of the cover around the poles at each corner (so it wouldn't fly away).

The tripod with four legs also had a spike on the top. This went in a hole right in the middle of the cover. There are four more poles, each with a slight angle near one end. He connected one of these poles to one of the four legs, then lifted it up to form a peaked roof. He attached the other end of the pole to a corner. He did the same thing with the other three poles, and the awning was up.

He strapped the cover around the poles in several places. Then, he drove some large spikes into the ground and tied the poles to the spikes. They help keep the awning straight, and stop it from blowing away.

The setup guy got out a bin. Among other things, it contained a blue strip of cloth about a foot high and four feet wide with the mortuary's name on it. He attached this to the velcro at the front of the awning. Next he set up several ordinary folding chairs. He took a bunch of blue chair covers out of the bin. These also had the mortuary's name on them. He put the covers over the folding chairs, so they looked nice and had a soft seat. He set up a battery-powered speaker with a wireless microphone, tested the mic, and shut it off. Job done.

At this point, he texted the mortuary to let them know that everything was ready, and also where in the cemetery the awning was. Then he drove off to set up for another service a few miles away.

The company he works for serves ten different mortuaries in cities over a 75-mile range. If a mortuary has a funeral in another state, the company charges a bit extra to cover the cost of the fuel, and off they go.

Occasionally, a funeral-setup truck has come to the cemetery, set things up, then parked in the shade for the next few hours. I had always wondered why the setup guy didn't just go back to his base. However, if the base is a couple of hours away, it's a more efficient use of time and money to just stay here, because he's going to have to come back after the service to gather up all of his equipment. But that's another story.

* * * * *

The sod around the cross area was growing well, with much watering, except for three dead spots. The dead spots turned out to be red anthills. I found some ant-killing powder and got rid of the ants. The dead spots recovered.

I find insects all over the place. Bees are almost everywhere that flowers are. It's not uncommon for me to pull up a weed and have hundreds of black ants come boiling out. One time, a mouse ran over my hand. Another time, it was a daddy-long-legs spider. Mayflies and moths and ladybugs are found on walls and windshields. Spiders climb in cracks and corners.

One time, I was sitting and weeding on the edge of a retaining wall, with my feet dangling over the edge. Unbeknownst to me, there was a hornets' nest in the retaining wall. One of the hornets crawled inside my pant leg and stung me on the thigh. Not my favorite experience. I was very careful around that retaining wall, after that.

* * * * *

I spent several months trying to gather money. The crowdfunding website helped immensely. It took a lot longer than I had wanted and I didn't get as much money as I had hoped. I'm still immensely grateful to all of the people who contributed. It would have been impossible without them. I made up the difference with my tax refund, which was unusually large that year. I'm grateful that my husband was willing to go along with it.

Finding a stonemason also took a while. Many, if not most, stonemasons these days work for companies. A company either won't do a job this small, or will charge a high price for it. One of the masonry-supply companies had a list of independent stonemasons, so I worked my way down the list, asking if the mason could rebuild a natural-stone cross.

"Natural stone," in this case, refers to uncut rocks of all shapes and sizes, rather than bricks or paving stones, which have a uniform shape and size. The answer was no; although they would sometimes come and look at the cross, before saying no. They all could build walls or terraces with bricks and other fabricated materials. Working with natural stone is a different skill.

Next, I called a small masonry-supply store to see if they could recommend anyone. They knew three people. One said no, one said yes, and the third said he had an assistant who sometimes did side jobs. The one who said yes planned to rebuild the cross using rebar. The assistant turned out to be a man probably in his sixties who had been working with stone since he was in his teens. He knew exactly how to rebuild the cross and, as luck would have it, he also had the low bid.

The original cross had been built in the 1930s, when building guidelines were looser. The stonemason had gathered stones from the surrounding area, which was undeveloped mountain. Then, he had started with a cement base, and mortared the stones together up to about six feet. Then he mortared a two-foot by six-foot steel plate on top and added more stones to form the T part of the cross.

The problem was that it was all held together by mortar. The mortar worked quite well in the ordinary way of things, but didn't provide enough stability when somebody wrapped a chain around the cross and pulled it over with a pickup truck[1]. A stonemason who lived nearby put the cross back up several times, but eventually left it alone. (This was sometime in the 1970s.)

The current stonemason decided that nobody was going to pull over this cross.

[1] According to one of the neighbors.

* * * * *

Death is a part of life, as I said earlier. This is even more true for rabbits than it is for people because rabbits are at the bottom of the food chain. There's a reason that rabbits have so many babies.

I have seen near misses with hawks and cats, and the remains when a hawk didn't miss. Two days after they left the nest, nine baby rabbits were down to six.

One day, a year earlier, I had come in to find a dead rabbit in the garbage can. I asked what had happened. The supervisor said that someone had shot the rabbit. Then they had remorsefully brought it to him, apologized, and said they would never do it again.

On the day the babies left the nest, I was watering a flowerbed by the office. I twitched the hose aside as I noticed a small white rabbit in the flowers. Then I realized it wasn't moving. It was dead. There wasn't a mark on it, but a wasp was hovering nearby, which might have stung it. I carefully wrapped it in a paper towel and took it around to the back of the office.

A woman and three children were there. They had come to see the rabbits. I pointed out Mama Rabbit and told them they could look around for the babies. Then I slipped my nearly weightless bundle into the garbage can. A few minutes later, a little girl went running past the flowerbed where I had been watering.

A couple of days later, I came in to find the rabbits conspicuously absent. Someone had taken them home, to protect the babies from the hawks. They returned about three weeks later and were dispersed around the cemetery. (But not by the office.)

Once I had found a stonemason to rebuild the cross, he immediately set to work, to meet the Memorial Day deadline. Sometime earlier, the supervisor had dug a three-foot hole with the backhoe, at my request.

The stonemason sunk some rebar into the hole and partially filled it with concrete. Then he stacked pairs of cinder blocks up to about six feet to form a frame. The rebar went through the holes in the cinder blocks. Then he filled the holes with concrete.

He had the two-foot by six-foot steel plate sandblasted (to clean the rust off) and given a waterproof coating. He also had a couple of six-inch pieces of rebar welded to the plate. He put the plate on top of the cinder blocks at the time he put the concrete in, with the rebar facing down. When the concrete cured, the plate was an integral part of the structure.

While the lead stonemason was working with rebar and cinder blocks, his partner was disassembling the old cross. He knocked the stones loose with a sledge hammer. They also had the rocks that I had brought from the mountain. I had cleaned the black spray paint off of the cross shortly after we moved it.

When the cinder-block frame was ready, they wrapped it with chicken wire. They also hung string at all four corners as vertical reference lines, to show where the stone needed to reach. Then they got started. They would take a piece of stone, mortar it, place it, and then wire it to the chicken wire. That held it in place long enough for the mortar to dry. After the mortar dried, they cut off the wire.

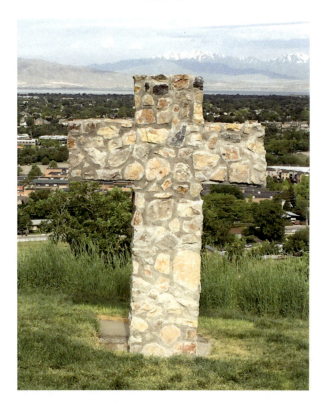

They covered the cross with a tarp when they left for the night, so the sprinklers wouldn't soak it.

The stonemasons set up scaffolding as the work went higher. They also made a cinder-block frame on top of the steel plate for the crosspiece.

They worked evenings and weekends because they both had day jobs. I stopped by every day to see how the work was progressing. They finished the Easter Cross by the deadline, a few days before Memorial Day, 2017.

After it had cured for a few days, they used an acid wash to make the colors brighter. They also added a waterproof coating. The lead stonemason did some research and said that this was the only masonry cross in the United States.

They did a darn good job; one to be proud of. I was really impressed with their skill, workmanship, and work ethic. A forgotten monument was restored and visible for all to see.

* * * * *

I spend about half of my time watering plants. I hook up a hose near the office and water the potted plants by the door and several other sections that I can reach with the hose. I fill up two watering cans and bring along the hose (just in case), and drive the battery-powered cart to the hill south of the office. It has only a few plants, so I use the watering cans. It's not worth hooking up the hose. Then I drive east toward the wall of pyracantha bushes. (Pyracanthas are very dense, very prickly, and at some times of the year have clusters of orange berries.)

This area has a lot of plants. The upper part has half a dozen caryopteris shrubs that need watered, and the lower part has some salvia, beebalm, primroses, and a few other things. This one calls for the hose.

There's usually already a hose somewhere in the area, complete with a sprinkler and the spigot that allows me to hook into the underground

water system. If there isn't one, I use the one I brought along. I refill the watering cans while I'm there. Then I head to the far northwest corner.

This is where the Easter Cross is. I use one of the watering cans to water the plumbago and the newly planted St. John's wort because the nearest hose hookup is a couple of levels higher. I also water the plumbago and sedum planted in the rock retaining wall. Then I drive south to the flagpole.

The flagpole is bordered by lilies and chrysanthemums and the north part is out of range of the sprinklers. I make sure all of the plants have water. Then I head back toward the office. I stop along the way to empty the rest of the first watering can onto a butterfly bush that I'm trying to revive.

Then I take the cart back to the office and plug it in to recharge the battery, while I get on with the rest of my work (primarily weeding).

One morning, I was watering south of the office when I spotted a large flock of wild turkeys ambling through the grass. There were about two dozen of them, half adults and half young ones. I watched them for a bit and then went over by the pyracantha bushes, where there are usually three or four rabbits, hopping around and nibbling at the grass.

As I was watering the upper part of the garden, two of the rabbits came bounding out of the pyracantha bushes. They stopped in the grass, but sat there alert with their ears sticking straight up. Several seconds later, a large orange cat came out of the bushes. It strolled after the rabbits, who kept well ahead of it. It eventually

gave up and wandered off to the west, away from the bushes.

I was watering the lower part of the area when I heard a tremendous gobbling noise. I turned around to see that the cat had gone after the turkeys. It was sitting on a ledge, looking rather taken aback, with two or three turkeys nearby. I think the turkeys had spotted the cat and sounded the alarm, then moved between it and their young ones. The cat slunk off down the hill and the turkeys resumed their grazing.

* * * * *

After watching the funeral setup, I wanted to watch the other side of things: sealing the vault and closing the grave. I had some trouble because I leave work around noon and most funerals don't start until at least 11. So I watched the schedule and found a service on a Saturday and came in then.

I decided to weed a hill that was a couple hundred yards from the awning, but still offered a good view of the area and the parking lot. About half an hour before things started, a mortuary representative came and checked the area and made sure everything was ready. He also carried a large cluster of balloons over to the grave site.

About 20 minutes later, a big white van came in and parked at the edge of the road. Some other mortuary reps had brought flowers from the funeral, which they placed around the grave site. The lawn is pretty big, and this grave was out in the middle of it, so they had a bit of a walk.

Finally, a long black hearse drove into the cemetery, followed by a stream of cars. My hill was close to the turnoff from the driveway into the cemetery, so I got a good look. The road forks right there, so the full-timers put up a sign that says "Service today" and points the direction where the cars need to go.

For the next several minutes, people were arriving and unloading, but finally they were ready. A violin played a medley of "Amazing Grace" and "Come Thou Fount of Every Blessing," while the pallbearers carried the casket from the road to the grave site.

I had worked far enough south on the hill that the awning was obscured by the pyracantha bushes, but I could still hear male voices singing, "God Be With You 'Til We Meet Again," followed by the measured tones of someone offering a prayer. A few minutes later, the family released a great cloud of blue and white balloons into the sky. Shortly after that, the hearse and the big white van drove away.

I started watching the funeral-setup truck, which had been parked unobtrusively in a corner since before the service had started. I figured the driver would know when to move in. The family was in no hurry (and they shouldn't have been. Waiting for them is part of our job.).

I had time to finish the hill, double check that I hadn't missed anything, dump the weeds in the compost pile, watch some children chase the rabbits, and sit in my car for a bit before the grave site was empty of people. At that point, the setup truck moved in.

* * * * *

Encounters with Rabbits

I was watering the plants in the southeast corner of the cemetery, as usual. Three rabbits were out, also as usual; a white one, a tan one, and a white one with black ears. Most of the time, the rabbits are quietly grazing on the lawn. Not today.

The tan one and the black-eared one were lying under a bush. The white one came charging in, tripped, and recovered. Then it ran toward the bush. It chased the black-eared one around the bush a few times. The black-eared one ran away, and the white one flopped under the bush.

The brown one ran around for a bit and flopped back under the bush. The black-eared one came back, and the white one chased it around the bush again. The black-eared one came back a few more times, and was chased around the bush. It finally went and hid in the trees. The other two eventually followed. I finished up with the watering.

* * * * *

I was cleaning the cemetery bathroom, like I usually do on Monday morning. The bathroom is on the south side of the office and is accessible from the outside. A lot of people come to the cemetery over the weekend. We frequently have funeral services on Saturday.

The cemetery is closed on Sunday, but the gate stays open, so people come in and walk around. Sometimes they have family gatherings, or just walk along the roads. The cemetery has lots of trees and bushes, so there's plenty of shade and benches to sit on. The view from the west side is spectacular. You can see over Provo and Orem and past Utah Lake to the mountains on the far side of the valley.

Two rabbits were munching on the lawn as I walked from the supply closet inside to the bathroom outside. I cleaned the mirror, toilet, and sink, and was working on the floor when I noticed I had company. A brownish-gray rabbit had come to investigate.

It hopped from the grass to the cement pad outside the door. Then it hopped inside the bathroom and started examining my boots. I offered it my fingers, like I would to a dog, and its whiskers tickled my fingers as it sniffed. Then it went back outside to eat the grass again.

* * * * *

From the time we had cleared the land where the cross would go, a clump of scrub oak

had been begging for a bench. The trees were perfectly situated for someone to sit in the shade and look out over the valley. For quite a while, a bench was fairly low on the priority list because we had to do the landscaping and get the cross reconstructed. But, eventually, the time seemed right.

Just about every bench in the cemetery has a family name engraved on it. Some also have poetry or pictures or scriptural quotes. Most of the benches look the same. They have a rectangular piece of polished gray granite placed on two square pieces of polished gray granite; kind of like Stonehenge, but at sitting height. A few have different colors of granite or a back on the bench.

My first step was to talk to the sexton, who is in charge of plots and benches and other such things. It seems that everyone wants to have a family bench; so EastLawn Cemetery has a rule that a family must own at least nine plots before they can buy a bench. The family then pays a fee for the land that the bench will sit on, and orders the bench from one of the local monument companies.

Since I had the land for the cross, I didn't need to worry about the nine plots or the fee. I asked the sexton if I had to order a specific kind of bench. She said no. There are just so many of the gray granite benches that everyone thinks it's required.

I talked to a local monument company to get some prices. It turns out that the cheapest type of bench is... a gray granite bench. Changing the color increases the price. Changing the shape or adding a back also increases the price. The engraving is included at no extra cost.

That bench style may have been the cheapest, but it was out of my price range, and the people whom I asked to sponsor it declined.

It occurred to me around then that I didn't need to get a granite bench. It wasn't required by the cemetery and the Easter Cross is off in its own corner anyway, so I didn't need to worry about matching. I looked into benches that were comfortable to sit on.

I decided on a Wingline-style bench. It's a contoured bench with a back, and made of slats so any rain or snow will just run off of it. It also cost less than half of what a granite bench did.

I showed the design to the owner who not only approved it, but also offered to split the cost. At that point, it was fairly easy to get half-a-dozen people to help with the remaining cost.

Encounters with Rabbits

I ordered a green bench with black posts, to fit with the outdoor ambience.

It arrived disassembled, wrapped in plastic, and strapped to a pallet. The supervisor used a forklift to move it out of the way until I could arrange to install it. But that's another story.

* * * * *

Contrary to popular belief, rabbits do not live on carrots. They eat grass, chrysanthemums, primroses, beebalm, and just about anything they can get their teeth on. (Although they tend to leave vinca and St. John's wort alone.) It is very annoying to plant some new flowers and come back a few days later to find them eaten down to stubs. The deer are nearly as bad, but they go for higher and larger plants. We spread nylon mesh over the plants to protect them from the nibblers.

One day, I was out weeding an area when I realized that the nylon mesh over the strawberries was gone. (We had planted the strawberries at the request of a mother whose baby was buried nearby.) I looked around, trying to see where it had walked off to. As it turned out, it hadn't walked. It had slithered. A large brown-and-tan snake was completely tangled up in the mesh. It was about four feet long and as thick as my thumb.

I checked the color—brown and tan, not red and black—and the tail—smooth, no rattles—and decided it was harmless. (A neighbor later identified it as a blow snake, or gopher snake.) The snake could flex its coils, but it couldn't straighten out, so it couldn't go anywhere. It was not getting out of that mesh without help.

I picked up the snake by the mesh and moved it out of the flowerbed and onto the grass. I unwrapped about a third of the snake, but the rest of it was woven through the mesh. I went back to the office for a pair of scissors[1].

The snake hadn't gone anywhere. I held it with one hand while I carefully worked the scissors between its skin and each strand of the mesh. I kept an eye on its head to be sure it wouldn't bite, but the head was covered by the mesh. All the snake could do was watch me and hiss a little.

I worked my way up its body until I had freed another third of the snake. It took off toward the flowerbed, but it was still trailing a huge wad of mesh, so it didn't get very far. I moved it back to the grass. I tried to keep an eye on its head, but it had coiled up tightly with its head at the bottom of the pile. I continued to work my way up the snake.

Encounters with Rabbits

I had cleared everything but a piece of mesh about the size of my hand, when the snake took off again. It slithered across the lawn and hid under a bush. I let it go. If the mesh got caught, the snake could work its way out of it, and I really didn't want to dive into a bush after a snake.

I put the biggest piece of mesh back over the strawberries. Then, I put the scissors in my pocket and the rest of the mesh in the trash and got back to work. For the next several minutes, I heard a very loud "SSSSSSSSSSSSS," as the snake announced its displeasure to the world.

[1] I wish I had thought to grab my camera right then, but I didn't. I haven't seen the snake before or since.

* * * * *

One day, I was watering as usual, and the big flock of wild turkeys was wandering through the cemetery. A few minutes later, I heard a great fuss among the turkeys and they all took to the air. Some of them landed in the trees nearby and others flew even farther.

I went to see what had disturbed them. A bobcat? A person? No. A big friendly dog.

* * * * *

After the family had left the grave site, the funeral-setup truck moved from the corner where it had been waiting to the part of the road closest to the site. The driver got out and walked over to the grave site. He was a lot younger than the other driver I had watched. I went over and asked if I could watch. He said yes. I asked if he was allowed to bring a book with him. He laughed and said he was a student, so he mostly brought homework.

He started by removing the roller bars from under the casket. (There were three.) Then he set aside the flowers on top of the casket. One of the corners of the casket-lowering device has a knob sticking up and a lever on one side. The lever is a lock that keeps the poles from turning and unrolling the straps.

He took a crank out of his pocket and placed it over the knob. Then he released the lever, and turned the crank a few times to get the mechanism going. The mechanism lowers the casket into the vault at a steady pace. Once it was down, we worked the straps out from under the casket. He said that the vault had some supports in the middle, so the straps weren't pinned under the casket.

We straightened the straps and he turned the poles of the casket-lowering device to tighten the straps. Then he moved the lever to lock them in place. We picked up the casket-lowering device and carried it off to the side. Then we moved the device supports; the previous setup guy had four separate supports. This one had two connected together at each end. We folded up the greens, which had dead grass and leaves on the bottom. I asked if we needed to clean

them. He said he would clean them with a shop vac when he got back to the office.

While the setup guy and I were gathering the chair covers, moving the folding chairs, and disassembling the awning, the full-timers were placing plywood on the headstones between the road and the grave site. Then the setup guy drove the truck over to the grave site and backed up to the grave. He positioned one of the outriggers on the plywood and another on a piece of wood.

This setup truck was simpler than the other one. Instead of a four-hook chain, he had a big, heavy strap that he looped through the top-left and bottom-right handles of the lid. He placed the ends of the strap over the hook of the crane. When he lifted it, the lid was off-center but it stayed where it needed to be. The crane did not have a remote control. The driver stood at the truck and manipulated the controls there. He moved the lid over the vault (which was painted a beautiful copper color) and I turned it so it lined up properly. Then he lowered it into place.

We picked up the aluminum planks that laid along the sides of the vault and put them on the back of the truck. This truck did not have cabinets. At the head and foot of the hole were some boards that looked like railroad ties.

Unlike the steel vault supports of the other truck, which ran crosswise, this one had two steel cables that ran lengthwise. Both cables had a loop at each end. The loops poked up through holes in the railroad tie and were held there by a three-foot metal spike. The cables ran under the vault and up through two holes in the other railroad tie, and were held by a similar spike.

The setup guy looped two steel cables around the ends of the vault and then attached them to the hook on the crane. When he raised the crane, the friction of the cables lifted the vault. He had me remove one of the three-foot metal spikes, which released the support cables. He then lowered the vault into the hole. When it was down, he climbed down in the hole and unhooked the friction cables from around the vault. Then, we pulled the support cables out of the hole.

Next, he used the crane to move a flat steel rack, which was about the length and width of a vault, from the back of the truck to the ground. He loaded all of his gear onto the rack. Railroad ties, cables, chairs, greens, chair covers (in a duffle bag), awning (in an army rucksack), casket-lowering device, supports, and all. Then he used the crane to lift the rack back onto the

truck. He returned the crane to its traveling position, raised the outriggers, thanked me, and went on his way.

* * * * *

A few times a week, the monument people come to the cemetery to place (or replace) headstones on the graves. Like the funeral-setup people, they drive a truck with a crane, but the crane is centered over the back of the truck, rather than placed at the corner of the passenger side. They can carry multiple headstones at a time.

After finding the correct location, a monument guy backs the truck into position and lowers the headstone into place. Once it's positioned exactly, they draw a line around it. Then the crane moves the headstone out of the way. They cut the sod from around the area and place it on a tarp that is spread on the ground. Most headstones are four or five inches thick, so they dig a hole deep enough to hold it. They pile the dirt on the tarp so it doesn't mess up the grass. They level the bottom of the hole so it's perfectly flat.

Once the hole is ready, they use the crane to lift the headstone into position. They fill dirt around the edges of the headstone so it is snug. Then they use a broom to sweep the dirt off the headstone, and make sure it looks nice. They use the crane to lift the tarp, dirt and all, into the back of the truck. Then, they're off to lay the next headstone.

* * * * *

After the bench was ordered and delivered, it needed to be installed in the cross area. The mounting options for the bench had been in-ground, surface mount (with bolts into concrete), or portable (free-standing). Given the location, I went with in-ground. I could assemble the bench easily enough, but I knew very little about concrete. So I went looking for help.

One of my neighbors is a handyman and knows a thing or three about concrete, so I asked him for help. Among other things, he said I needed to get two 18-inch by two-and-a-half foot sonotubes to hold the concrete. I took careful notes and then went online to figure out what he was talking about.

A sonotube is basically a very large, strong cardboard tube that is treated to hold concrete. The local home-improvement store carried a few, but its largest was 12 inches, and I needed 18. I started calling industrial supply stores.

Encounters with Rabbits

They had 18 inches, but the shortest was 10 feet long. They were willing to cut it to size, so I figured I would take home the extra five feet.

That went pretty well as planned, except for fitting a five-foot by 18-inch tube into a four-door car. (Small cars are less than five feet wide.) I ended up laying the passenger-side seat completely back, but we managed to get it to fit. (The smaller pieces fit in the trunk.) Then I drove home very carefully because I could only see my driver's side mirror.

I called my local expert again and we figured out how much concrete we would need. We discussed several options on how to get the concrete to the cross area. We decided to buy concrete mix and rent an electric mixer from the home-improvement store. He offered to pick up the materials in his truck. I accepted gratefully. (I repaid him for the materials later.) We decided to do the installation on Saturday.

After lunch on Friday, I went over to the cemetery to collect everything we would need, and dig a couple of three-foot holes for the sonotubes. We wanted the tops of the tubes to be below ground level. The weather was sunny and cool. It took about twenty minutes of measuring and observing to determine the spots for the sonotubes. I wanted them under the trees, but positioned to have a good view. Then I traced around them so I knew how big to make the holes.

The holes took a while. The full-timers run the sprinklers fairly regularly, so the ground was soft (I asked them not to run the sprinklers until Monday), but after about two feet, I had trouble getting the dirt out of the hole. A shovel spills the dirt when the hole is that deep.

One of the guys came over to check on things and told me about a tool they have for extracting dirt, called a post-hole digger. I finished the hole fairly quickly once I got that. I dumped all the dirt by the edge of the grass, where I wanted to raise the ground level.

The second hole had scrub-oak tree roots. Lots of them. Loppers won't work below about a foot, because you can't open them far enough to get the jaws around the root. I mostly used the shovel and a big metal pry bar with a wedge at the end to chop the roots. Shovels are very good choppers. I also used a saw. I stopped around 5:00 to take care of things at home. Then, I came back and dug until dark, but I was still about six inches short when I had to quit.

My son and I came back around 9:00 Saturday morning (cool and sunny) and finished the hole. Then, the supervisor got the bench from where

it had been sitting for the past several weeks and hauled it over by the cross. We assembled the bench and hauled off the packing material. About then, my local expert showed up (with his dog, who wandered around and observed the proceedings). I directed him down to the cross.

We spent about half an hour unloading, and running extension cords and hoses, and moving the bench out of the way, and dodging a graveside service, which had started about then up on the main level. Then we got to work.

We leveled the sonotubes and placed several rocks at the bottom of the hole (to reduce the amount of concrete needed), and mixed and poured the cement.

After the sonotubes were full, my neighbor placed a couple of rocks and two-by-fours as scaffolding and we put the bench into the cement. He then spent about 15 minutes making sure the bench was level, and the right height and the right angle, and propped it in place with rocks.

Then we covered the bench with a tarp, cleaned everything up, put everything away, and went home. It was about 3:00. The sky was overcast, but it didn't start raining until after we were finished.

On Monday morning, I removed the tarp and the scaffolding and tested out the bench. It was quite comfortable. I filled in the gap between the edge of the holes and the sonotubes. We hadn't done it before because the dirt might have spilled into the concrete. Then I covered the sonotubes with dirt and leveled the ground under the bench. Job done.

THANK YOU

EastLawn Memorial Hills Cemetery	Stonemasons:
Sundberg-Olpin Mortuary	Kevin Titcomb
Provo Community Congregational United Church of Christ	Jeremy Rohwer
Ellis Erosion Control	Jeremy Warner

* * * * *

People sometimes ask how I managed to restore the Easter Cross, when nobody else had been able to. Part of it is my nature. I'm very persistent. I'm like the tortoise in the fable of the tortoise and the hare. I tend to be slow, but when I tackle a project, I don't give up until it's done. (This means that I'm pretty selective about which projects I tackle.)

The other part is that, from the beginning, I had the distinct feeling that God wanted the Easter Cross back up. If God wants something done, it will get done. I knew if I just kept going, things would eventually fall into place. I did quite a bit of praying, and some fasting, especially to find a location.

Whenever I ran into a roadblock or metaphorical brick wall, I would ask God, "Are you sure you want this cross up?" The answer was always yes. So I would sigh and rack my brains and look around some more, and try to think of something I hadn't tried yet. Things would eventually work out, and I would continue onward until I ran into the next roadblock.

While I was the driving force, I could not and did not do this alone. Many people gave their time, money, labor, equipment, etc. to make this project possible. I made a bronze plaque for the major contributors.

EastLawn Cemetery provided the location. Sundberg-Olpin Mortuary made a major financial contribution. The Provo Community Congregational United Church of Christ made the fundraising possible. Ellis Erosion Control moved the cross.

Thank you, everyone. This would not have happened without you.

* * * * *

The cemetery has a lot of vehicles: Backhoes, dump trucks, trailers, the small white pickup, the battery-powered Polaris ranger, ATVs, and a bicycle.

One trailer is for hauling dirt, branches, trash, and other such things. Another trailer is enclosed and holds the cemetery's greens, awning, folding chairs, seat covers, and casket-lowering device.

The supervisor will sometimes use the bicycle when he needs to get to or from a backhoe that's parked far away. He rides the bicycle over, puts it in the loader of the backhoe, and drives the backhoe back. Other times, he'll drive the backhoe over with the bicycle in the loader, and ride back.

All of the vehicles are used fairly regularly, but the one that gets the most use is probably the small white pickup. I believe the cemetery bought it as surplus from the local university

(since the university logo is still on the door). It is a 15-year-old Ford Ranger that is much the worse for wear.

It is used to haul just about everything: Hand tools, power tools, gas cans, leaves, branches, sod, 4×8-foot sheets of plywood, and dirt. It is not street legal (its maximum speed is about 25 mph), but it goes almost everywhere in the cemetery.

The fact that it still runs is a testament to the supervisor's skill with machines. It used to have an automatic transmission. Now it has a steel rod that passes through a slit in the floor and hooks directly to the engine. The rod can be all the way back (park), a few inches forward (reverse), or all the way forward (drive). The key disappeared a while back, so the supervisor removed the safety lock and now we start it with a screwdriver.

The seats are torn, the back window is missing, the tail gate is gone, the tail lights are broken, and holes are rusted through the bed in a few places. The radio works, sometimes. The windshield wipers work, but the turn signals just make a buzzing noise.

The truck has manual windows, fortunately, or we probably wouldn't be able to move them. It seems pointless to roll up the side windows to keep the rain (or sprinklers) out, when the back window is completely gone. But it works, more often than not.

The truck has been around the cemetery for longer than I have, and may still be there when I'm gone.

* * * * *

Encounters with Rabbits

Winter brings different work to the cemetery. The services continue, as usual, but there's no mowing or watering to be done. We do some of the things that we don't have time for during the summer; like thoroughly clean the office and trim dead branches off the trees.

Snow adds some extra work. First, the full-timers have to clear it away from the grave site so they can make sure they are digging in the right place. Then, they clear a path from the grave site to the road, so the funeral goers don't have to wade through the snow.

One January morning, I came in to find the supervisor pounding the backhoe bucket on the ground like a pile driver. He needed to dig a grave, but the ground was frozen solid. The water in the ground had turned to ice.

The full-timers use a mattock and a shovel to make a groove around the grave site, about an inch deep. Then, they fill the groove with hot, salty water. The water thaws the ground, and the salt keeps the water from freezing.

They can eventually remove a strip of sod and dirt that's about a foot long, and as wide as the grave. Then they bang the teeth of the backhoe bucket about a foot back from the edge to break off large chunks of dirt. The groove acts like scoring and makes the grass break off evenly. Once they're past the frost line (frozen part), they can dig as usual.

The rabbits are still around in the winter. They come out of the pyracantha bushes to nibble the grass. The deer come down more often to find food. The whole world waits for the coming of spring.

* * * * *

So that's what it's like at the EastLawn Cemetery. There are some variations. The funeral-setup truck isn't always needed, like when somebody opts to be cremated or chooses a polymer vault. A cremation urn can be easily carried by hand. A polymer vault can be carried by two people. At those times, the cemetery's awning and chairs are set up.

On one memorable occasion, the grave site was on the side of a hill, where the backhoe couldn't reach. The full-timers got to dig a double-deep hole by hand with shovels.

Another time, the hole was unstable so the vault and awning were set up some distance away so the ground wouldn't collapse under the funeral-goers. On another occasion, the full-timers came in at 5:30 in the morning, because the family wanted the funeral before sunrise.

The Easter Cross stands in its own private place. It's in the northwest corner of the cemetery with a view of the whole valley. It has a comfortable bench for people to sit and admire the view. The area is high enough and far enough from everything that even the occasional sound of traffic isn't really disruptive.

The rabbits come and go. Sometimes there are more, and sometimes less. Having one show up while I'm working never gets old.

Although every city has a cemetery, I think I can safely say that EastLawn Cemetery is one of a kind.

THE END

ACKNOWLEDGMENTS

I would like to thank everyone who helped with the publication of this book.

Thanks to Sky Evans for such an awesome cover and to Matt Wright for his help with the layout. Also, thanks to Gary Thornock, Rebecca Thornock, Paul and Sherryl Crockett, and Salvador Lopez for reading various drafts of the book and offering feedback.

Thanks to my family for their patience with and support of yet another project. Thanks to C. for his help with all sorts of things. Finally, thanks to K., who kept asking for bunny stories and helped me realize that other people might like them too.

ABOUT THE AUTHOR

Niki Thornock has lived in Provo, Utah since 1989. She and her husband have three children. In addition to working at EastLawn Cemetery, she is a part-time freelance editor. She has cowritten a 300-page ward history of the area at the foot of Y Mountain, and collected a newspaper trail of the creation of Provo's Kiwanis Park. She enjoys reading, karate, and computer games.